HOW GOD GIVES US
APPLES

By Mary LeBar

Illustrated by Kathryn Hutton

ISBN: 0-87239-357-7

 STANDARD PUBLISHING
Cincinnati, Ohio   3627

Away inside a big red apple

God made a little brown seed.

Down it fell to the dark, damp earth,
The home God knew it would need.

Sun

and rain

made the little seed sprout.

Up in the air it grew.

It spread its branches
wide and high
as apple trees
like to do.

There were little green leaves
and pretty pink flowers.

That grew on each bending bough.

And where the flowers were once so gay

there were little green apples now.

The little green apples grew larger
and larger
until they were big and round.

When the sunshine kissed them, the green turned

red.

And the ripe ones
fell to the ground.

Now you know how apples grow.
Thank you, God, for apples.